Old CATRINE & SORN

by
Rhona Wilson

CATRINE SCHOOL.   PHYSICAL DRILL.

Pupils taking part in a military style drill at Catrine Public School, built on the garden of Dugald's farmhouse. Stewart Place can be seen in the background.

© Stenlake Publishing 1997
First Published in the United Kingdom, 1997
By Stenlake Publishing, Unit 16A, Thistle Business Park North,
Ayr Road, Cumnock, Ayrshire KA18 1EQ
Telephone/fax: 01290 423114

ISBN 1 872074 91 X

Introduction

Some villages and towns were developed by the Industrial Revolution - Catrine was created by it. With only two or three cottages it was barely a hamlet in the mid-1780s; nearby Sorn was a metropolis in comparison. Catrine's name derived not from its first settlers but from nomadic bandits who included the area in their territory. 'Cateran' means 'robber' or 'cattle-lifter' and refers to the marauders who ran lucrative protection rackets - extracting a 'toll' for safe passage - along the nearby drove route, the Pass of Balloch. This all changed dramatically with the return in 1786 of one Claud Alexander from India, who, in a gesture of half paternalism and half modernism, set up the Catrine Mills.

Ballochmyle estate had been acquired by friends of Sir Claud in his absence and having the aristocratic home all he needed next was the aristocratic industry. He was lucky enough to meet up with David Dale who had established the New Lanark mills the previous year and was an expert in the technology as well as an ambitious and energetic improver. The two formed a partnership and built two mills, initially to provide warp and weft yarn for hand-loom weavers. Just over ten years later a factory community of around 1,300 with its own tailor-made village surrounded the premises. Most of these workers were incomers but, considering Catrine's self-containment, it's doubtful anyone complained. The new industry benefited its rural and agricultural neighbours by providing a ready market for their produce as well as alternative employment.

Although Alexander had laid the foundations, it wasn't until the mills were sold, still in their infancy, that the most startling technological developments began to take place. Kirkman Finlay & Co. took over in 1801 and initiated a period of intense innovations culminating in the Big Wheel. Archibald Buchanan, former apprentice to Sir Richard Arkwright, inventor of power spinning machinery, was brought into the company and the first of the new improvements was the creation of dams at Glenbuck the following year to ensure the supply of water. By 1805 power loom weaving had been introduced, beginning the slow strangle of hand-loom weaving. 1820 saw the establishment of the bleachworks which made big savings in time, space and money, and seven years later Buchanan had the revolutionary 200 horse power Big Wheel installed within its own wheelhouse. Seventy years later it was still on the map as a tourist phenomenon for Victorian coach parties.

Like everywhere else Catrine suffered a slump in demand after the end of the Napoleonic Wars in 1815. These had been a huge source of business in terms of army blankets and uniforms, particularly for hand-loom weavers, and a few years earlier Buchanan, by then manager, was being urged by Finlay to get armed protection after hand-loomers attacked machinery at his Deanston plant. It wasn't until the 1830s that the factory suffered its first real strike when workers, agitated by the Reform and Chartist movements, demanded the formation of a union and better wages. The strike failed and was supposedly resolved amicably.

Considering the village's financial dependence on the company and the comparative ease of conditions, anything else would have been surprising.

In many ways Catrine must have seemed a charmed world. Its streets had gas lighting four years before London. Services such as maintenance of the church, water supply and sewage collection were organised by the Feuars of Catrine, courtesy of the company. Mill workers were charged cheap rents for their houses which they could buy if they wished and a free education was provided in the company schoolhouse. Horizons were broadened further when the rail station eventually arrived in 1903. Certainly, the Catrine workers seemed more progressive in their attitudes than their neighbours in Sorn; most Catrine parents innoculated their children which was definitely not the case in nearby villages. But for this enlightenment and the good conditions, mill workers had to pay. They faced a minimum twelve hour day yoked to the factory system and the everlasting loss of the independence which was the main advantage of the alternative agricultural work. And since the mills were the main source of work in Catrine for going on two centuries, their descendants were stuck with this way of life too.

The boom couldn't last forever. Although Catrine escaped the ravages of the twenties and thirties suffered by towns dependent on mining, by the 1950s Britain's cotton industry was in dire straits. Finlays built the new mill to replace the Mule Mill and weaving sheds at the start of the decade, hoping to keep at the forefront of technology. The company experimented with colour and new products and opened Finlay Boutiques in department stores. But it was no use. Catrine couldn't compete with cheap imports and man-made fibres. Lack of government assistance didn't help either and the closure of the railway in the early forties had brought back the perennial problem of transport costs. Perhaps, too, the problem was partly cultural. Finlays prided itself on its special stamp signifying a life-time guarantee - but who wanted a tablecloth to last a lifetime with the advent of consumerism?

The bleachworks soldiered on until the seventies but the original mill closed in the early sixties; not long afterwards the huge premises disappeared. Up for demolition, the mills were felled instead by an accidental fire - at least they went out in style. The site was cleared to become a dubiously designed square surrounded by luridly painted tenements. A new business has appeared on site in the form of an optical factory, but it is a far cry from the noisy, swarming chaos of the former mill town. Despite Catrine's present drabness, what it was left with after the demise of the mills wasn't so different from the situation at New Lanark, now a prosperous tourist town. The village tells a particularly human tale of lost opportunities and impermanence. Despite being once at the pinnacle of industrialism, Catrine has returned to where it began - as a small, rural settlement looking outwards for work and leisure. It is as if the mills, for all their longevity, had never existed.

Huge mill complexes such as at Catrine, pictured here in 1938, were the end result of innovations applied to the humble, domestic spinning wheel. Introduced around 1770, the first improvement was the two-handled wheel which allowed spinners to double their output. This was followed by the development of the spinning jenny, which could increase its owner's yarn production by thirty times. However, the invention which moved weaving into the factory was Arkwright's waterframe. This large machine produced strong cotton warps and needed water to power it which is why early mills like Catrine, Blantyre and New Lanark were built on fast-running rivers. Finally, came the invention of the mule which was an amalgamation of the best features of the jenny and the waterframe, and Watt's steam engine was used to run this in the factories from the last decade of the eighteenth century.

Catrine was set up in the 1780s by Sir Claud Alexander and David Dale with the relatively small ambition of providing warp and weft yarn for handloom weavers. This picture shows how far that ambition came. To the left of the chimney is the weft mill with the weaving sheds behind it, and behind these on the right is the rounded roof of the wheelhouse. On the left is the cylinder of Catrine's gas works which was lighting the streets years before Glasgow or London. In 1790 a further works building, the Jeanie factory, was erected and eventually the complex had enlarged and developed to such an extent that it could carry out everything from processing cotton to making up the finished article. Raw cotton went in at the Jeanie House and by a complicated route, via the subterranean carding department and St Cuthbert Street bleachworks, came out the other end as table-cloths, towels and sheets.

Mill Street, viewed through the mill gates at the turn of this century, when the village and mills were still a tourist attraction. In partnership with David Dale, Sir Claud was working with one of the most startling innovators of the Scottish cotton industry. Dale had been involved in setting up the mills at New Lanark and Blantyre and his contacts with inventors such as Macintosh (of raincoat fame) and Rouen of Papillion in France helped him to expand the breadth of production in his factories. The latter, for example, was brought over to introduce Turkey Red Dyeing (a method of dyeing cotton red) to Scotland at the Blantyre mills. Despite this, the most inventive changes at Catrine did not take place until after Dale and Alexander were no longer involved. Finlay & Co. took over in 1801 and, managed by Archibald Buchanan, began a series of dramatic improvements over the next thirty years.

Archibald Buchanan's Big Wheel crowned three decades of innovation. By the time of his appointment as manager, Buchanan had already patented the self-acting mule which allowed his looms to run faster than the average rate. In the mid-1820s he was convinced that he could increase the water power available to him if he replaced his wooden mill wheel with several iron wheels shackled together. His engineer thought he was mad but Buchanan got his way and his specially made wheel was installed a couple of years later. Originally, four yoked wheels were planned but the two pictured here were enough to give 200 horsepower - more than required and a stunning amount of power at the time. The wheel travelled at a noisy three revolutions per minute but was a romantic sight in sunny weather with the wheelhouse full of rainbows. It survived an amazing one hundred and twenty years until it was superseded by electric power in 1947.

ST CUTHBERT ST CATRINE.

The voes excavated at St Cuthbert Street allowed a steady flow of water to the Big Wheel and Catrine ensured its water supply with a reservoir system near Glenbuck. Sluices were opened at 6pm and the water travelled a twelve hour journey, via the lade, to start the Big Wheel first thing in the morning. At the time this picture was taken the street was still made up of single-storey thatched cottages; but these days the approach to St. Cuthbert Street is somewhat disappointing as the deep pool here is half covered with a grubby mess of reeds and bogland. However, a little further on are the voes which have recently been the lucky subject of a European funded footpath project and behind St Cuthbert Street today is a picturesque network of pools and walkways - the only place in the village where its past has been combined successfully with its present.

By the 1840s Catrine had a burgeoning population of well over 2,500, most of it dependent on the mills for work. Mill employees, such as the group here, worked from twelve to fourteen hours a day, six days a week. They were summoned to the mill for a 6am start by the company alarm clocks, a specially employed drummer and the mill bell. Unsurprisingly, the latter was known as Hornie's Bell, i.e. the Devil's Bell. Once the workers were in, it was a long day's slog in servitude to the looms and they were kept in check by a special tool which made sure they paid for any slackening off. In the works office was a double grandfather clock, now in Finlay's Glasgow office. One face told the time and the other was geared to the wheel system. If the hand on this was low it meant that the flow of water had been weak that day and everyone had to stay late to make up for lower productivity of the machinery.

Country textile mills such as Catrine employed a mostly female workforce for several reasons. For a start there weren't many jobs which required a male's physical strength once powerlooming was in its stride. Women were more nimble, cheaper and easier to discipline considering their traditional stay-at-home role. Children were even better. They were small enough to crawl under the machinery to clear away debris and, if caught at an early age, could be moulded into unquestioning factory workers. In the Twist Mill when the works were first opened and at the Jeanie a few years later over half the employees were between the ages of nine and twelve. Thirty odd years later the trend still hadn't changed and in 1819 the works were employing forty-four widows (and no doubt their attendant children).

Workers in the Pillow Case Cutting Room - obviously not a female concern. In the early years of the mill there was a relationship of mutual distrust between male workers and the mills. A factory regime required a rigid discipline that was unnecessary in traditional occupations.Farm labourers and domestic weavers worked long hard hours, but they did so in their own homes or in the fields. Hand-loomers could work into the night if they had spent time off during the day; and although landworkers slogged through their spring and summer they enjoyed a relatively lazy season in the winter. Men such as these considered mill work appropriate only for those of the poorhouse and only went there if they were desparate. However, their old working habits sometimes made them ineffective at the mill as a telling comment, regarding a highland recruit, from one of Catrine's mill managers attests: 'He never sits at ease at a loom, it is like putting a deer in the plough.'

This postcard was posted by one of the mill workers to a former colleague with the message: "This is the mill yard as it used to be. The present manager didn't like the place like this so the flowers are a thing of the past. The man standing among the flowers is Chisholm - he used to be the policeman in Catrine. Do you remember?" No doubt the manager in question was unpopular but this wasn't necessarily a problem under Catrine's comparitively enlightened regime. If a worker didn't like a supervisor he or she was supposedly allowed to transfer to a different department.

This picture of Catrine's chaotic washing machine department was taken as part of Finlay's catalogue contribution to the 1938 Empire Exhibition, held in Bellahouston Park. Exhibitions such as these evolved from London's Crystal Palace exhibition in the mid-nineteenth century. They epitomised the confidence of the Victorian age, celebrating industry, technology and new ideas in the only mass medium available to them at the time. In Glasgow's first International Exhibition you could watch a brolly being put together and then saunter over to the industrial rooms to take a look at some colliery workings. By 1938 with Britain on the brink of another world war the lavish displays from its own industries and those of its satellites served instead as a useful propoganda and confidence-boosting device. Perhaps, too, they represented a last chance of self-promotion for Finlay's who were heading towards the disasterous fifties.

This huge machine room full of automatic sheeting looms gives some idea of Catrine's scale. From this evidence, it is small wonder that the powerloom industry was accused of killing off domestic handloom weaving in the nineteenth century. However, the truth was more complicated. Initially, handloomers had benefitted from the improvements to spinning as there was an excess of yarn for them to weave and the flying shuttle also increased their looms productivity. The years between 1780 and 1815 were a boom period for them as the Napoleonic Wars hugely increased the demand for uniforms and blankets. However, powerlooms were introduced around the same time and these soon became the focus of the handloomer's frustrations when the end of the war caused a recession. For a time attacks on machinery were common throughout Scotland.

The handloomers were victims of their own success. Until the mid-1820s they could easily compete with power looms as handlooms could produce far more intricate work reasonably quickly. However, the industry was in crisis long before then and a national strike had been attempted in 1812. Handlooming was so easy to learn and offered such prosperity at the time that the market was flooded with incomers eager to get rich from a simple trade. Ironically, the Napoleonic Wars which had provided staple employment for so long exacerbated this situation when they ended as hoards of not-so-young men came back from the army and found they were unable to find work in any other field. The 1812 strike was an attempt to set minimum piece rates and restrict entry to the trade but it failed miserably when the union leaders were arrested. Thereafter, numbers entering the trade increased despite the downward gallop of wages.

NEW MILL, CATRINE.

B.6886.

Catrine's new mill, opened in 1950, was an attempt to put Finlay's back at the forefront of technology. The Big Wheel had been replaced by electricity a few years earlier and this building was an initially successful attempt by the company to implement new ideas and technology. It was a huge investment but almost as soon as it had opened the British cotton industry took a nosedive. Imports from undeveloped countries were far cheaper and new fashions were eschewing traditional fabrics in favour of dubious man-made materials such as polyester and crimpelene. In this climate where tower blocks were universally loved and draylon thought sexy, Catrine's heritage meant very little. The company tried to change with the times, but although they opened dinky boutiques and tried different colours they were selling the wrong product in the wrong fabric at the wrong price. The new building closed less than twenty years later.

16

Plans to demolish the defunct old mill went awry when a small bonfire in the mill yard, set to burn waste, got out of control. The main buildings caught ablaze, providing a bitter-sweet spectacle for its former employees who clustered around St Germain Street, Bridge Street and the Post Office corner to watch. The mill had been built on the only possible roadway through the village and the council took the opportunity to clear the remains of the car-carbunkle in the early sixties. Mill Street was realigned and the mill site preserved as a common square, albeit one designed in a contemporary style guaranteed to keep it empty. Car owners were happy even if no-one else was .

AYR STREET CATRINE.

Ayr Street's thatched cottages overlooking the river have long been replaced by a block of new flats snaking round into Wood Street which just don't have the same charm. Behind Ayr Street to the right of this picture is Catrine's War Memorial, situated high up on the braetops. Apparently some old timers have been finding its height a problem and have requested it be brought down to the village so they don't get a crick in the neck looking at it. Perhaps the real problem is that the steps up to the braetops were previously maintained by Finlay & Co. It's now dangerous to go up this way and a new path has been cut instead.

BALLOCHMYLE HOUSE, CATRINE

203/70

Ballochmyle was acquired by Sir Claud in the 1780s and remained the Alexander family residence until the turn of the twentieth century. Thereafter the mansion was let out until it was sold to the Department of Health as a hospital during the war. After the fighting ended it was used as a rescue centre for several disasters in the area. The few survivors of a 1948 air crash were brought to Ballochmyle as were over ninety victims from the Knockshinnoch Colliery disaster in New Cumnock. Over the past few years the hospital has been dramatically phased down as plans for its replacement at Cumnock have taken shape and the mansion house is now falling apart. The Georgian Society has expressed interest in restoring it but with the roof caved in the financial outlay would be phenomenal.

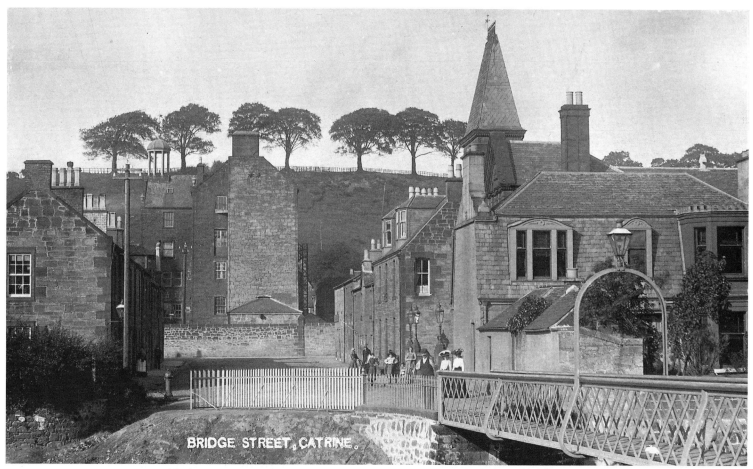

BRIDGE STREET, CATRINE.

Allowing access to the Institute, the Timm'er (Timber) Bridge was first opened as a wooden crossing in the 1870s. This became too flimsy for traffic and was replaced by a metal version that was cast in the mill yard. Many local men would have worked on maintenance or construction tasks such as this because their physical strength wasn't much in demand elsewhere. The Timm'er certainly kept them occupied - some years later it was swept away by floods and had to be replaced at a higher level. It looks much the same today, although the Victorian lamp has been removed. The turret on the right belongs to the Wilson Hall (used for concerts and as a cinema) which was built using a trust fund set up by local baker, John Wilson. Unfortunately he didn't leave enough money and a public subscription had to be set up to finish it. It was burnt down some time ago and replaced with an old folks' complex.

Catrine Bleachworks, up past St Cuthbert Street voes, opened in the 1820s and were a major economic development. Everything apart from bleaching was done in-house and this was one of the most costly phases of production. Cloth had to be either sent away which involved huge transport costs or bleached in fields by the unreliable Scottish sun which took up time and space. Nevertheless, the mill's own bleaching process was highly convoluted and took a couple of weeks, which was longer than its competitors. Extra costs were probably met by the works taking in bleaching from other companies but were worthwhile anyway due to the high quality finish the Finlay process gave. The works closed in the early seventies and have been used as a whiskey bond ever since.

Sorn Parish Agricultural Association was set up in the early 1870s and held an annual cattle show in Catrine which was a big social event for the surrounding villages. With few roads and primitive transport facilites, there weren't many opportunities to make the long journey by horse or foot to visit family and friends and the show was a way of killing two birds with one stone. Economically, it was to the advantage of most farmers to go and the bands and other amusements taking place were a draw for the community. It's possible that the moody bunch in the foreground of this picture belonged to Charlie Parker's Band, notorious in Catrine for the terrible jokes they inflicted upon their audience between tunes. The event pictured here was held at Park's field across the river from Holm Farm, which was another occasional venue for the show. Today the cattle show is mainly a business affair and has moved to Kingencleugh.

CATRINE COOP SOCY-LTD JUBILEE DAY

Before the first Co-ops were established in the 1820s, employers often owned the only shop in town and could charge whatever prices they liked. Co-ops, on the other hand, were run by the people for the people. Shopping at them was rewarded by an annual profit share in the form of a dividend which could be the equivalent of up to ten weeks wages. The Mill managers seemed reasonably amenable to the Catrine Co-op. The first, opened in the 1860s, was based in the works and the company provided room for a store when they moved to premises in the square. By the 1890s it had become prosperous enough to open a large multi-department store. Further investments by the society were made towards the houses of Co-op Avenue which were specifically built for the workers and they also provided food and drink for celebrations such as the local society's jubilee day, c.1910.

Daldorch House, Catrine.

Then known as Catrine Bank, Daldorch House was the residence of Archibald Buchanan, cousin to the Finlays and mill manager by 1807. An improver and inventor, Buchanan came from good stock. Legend has it that his father, James of Carston, was the first man north of the Forth to own a wheeled cart. Buchanan himself was apprenticed to Arkwright in his early teens, and he was sent off to the illustrious inventor with a herd of cows to pay for his keep. Although it looks fairly isolated here, the mansion house is just up past the voes and the former bleachworks and is reached by crossing a dilapidated bridge. Daldorch was bought in 1987 by the dubious sounding religious sect 'American Teen Mission', who were known mainly for their fleet of bicycles which were emblazoned with the name of the group - perhaps they were environmentalists. The house is presently being renovated into a school of some sort.

Gillies' general store was in a tenement block at the foot of the church steps which can be seen on the right. Next door to it was Milligan's Mansions and the Red Lion Inn was further along the road. These buildings became very dilapidated and were eventually demolished, the Red Lion (renamed as the Old Mill Inn) alone surviving.

One and a half miles from the centre of Catrine, the Howford Bridge links Mauchline with the outer areas of the town. It was built in 1750 around the same time as the nearby 'cup and ring markings' at Ballochmyle were graffittied. The bridge is still standing although the cottage to its right has disappeared. A story goes that an old tramp who died on the Catrine side of the bridge was hauled over to the Mauchline end by Catrine police called in to deal with his body. The Mauchline polis weren't quite so lazy and the tramp apparently has a grave in Mauchline Cemetary.

GALA DAY AT CATRINE.

CODONA'S MERRY-GO-ROUNDS.

In the nineteenth century there would have been little time for holiday events as mill workers only got around two days break a year, but by the 1940s the management were a little less stingy with the holiday allowance. Catrine's first carnival week was held in 1946 as part of the village's victory celebrations after the Second World War (the date of this picture is about 1910). The carnival was held in Town's Park which ran along Newton Street, but is all built up now.

Another Catrine Gala Day. Gala days and country events like the cattle show were at one time big crowd pullers for the Catrine workers but the event ceased some years ago. There was an attempt to revive it during the bicentenary year of 1987 but with no mill to bind it perhaps Catrine's community spirit was too weak to make it a success.

Mauchline Road, Catrine.

Catrine's first local authority housing was completed in the late twenties but Mauchline Road, originally called Ballochmyle Terrace, didn't appear until a couple of decades later. Recently, there has been talk of building on the nearby Burn Park but people are hopeful it won't happen. At the bottom of Mauchline Street begins Ballochmyle Street which once had a toll house to catch travellers along the turnpike road from Mauchline into the village. Before the advent of turnpikes, most roads were unmaintained dirt tracks and new private roads were often set up by a consortium of landowners as source of easy money.

Milk from Waukmill, Catrine

Mrs Stewart and her milk cuddie were a regular feature around Catrine in the early 1900s. The donkey's pannier's were filled with milk and eggs which Mrs Stewart sold around the village. She lived at the Waulkmill, opposite Daldorch, which was often flooded by the nearby river to the extent that it became a mini island. Apparently the donkey was often left to make its own way home because Mrs Stewart enjoyed a drink.

Mill Street, Catrine

JV 75546

Originally named Twist Mill Street, Mill Street had an open lade running down its middle till around 1904 and this accounts for its massive breadth here. Residents in Mill Street had the unsavoury habit of emptying their ash waste into the running water. The County Council planted trees in 1901 to act as a safety barrier but this wasn't enough as a drowning incident in 1902 proved. Sources disagree about whether the person actually died but the lade was considered a danger and eventually filled in. The boy on the pavement on the left marks the position of the Red Mill Inn which still stands. These days Mill Street has been greatly narrowed as a result of the mill being demolished.

ST. GERMAIN STREET, CATRINE

St Germain Street was named after the patron saint of weavers. The Brewery Bar on the left still exists as does the Bazaar building which supplied the village and the surrounding farms with groceries although it is now a private residence. At the far end of the street the concrete inlay around the mill entrance was added as a memorial to one of the mill's former managers. At the time of this picture, c.1910, Catrine's cotton crisis was just beginning and the mill would not last the depression. Unfortunately, there was little thought of preserving the buildings - in the 1960s anything that was new was valued over anything that was old and a lot of council's demolished their tenement buildings without a thought to conservation.

Before Catrine got its own railway station it had to rely on Mauchline's. The other town was on the main Kilmarnock - Dumfries line but goods could only be transported from Catrine by wagon. Navvies pictured here around the beginning of this century were working for the Glasgow and South Western Railway Company who filled in the gap. At Catrine the new lines allowed the mill access to the West of Scotland ports from which goods were exported. It also allowed villagers greater access to the outside world, making it easier to work elsewhere if they wished.

CATRINE STATION.
FIRST STEAM MOTOR CAR IN SCOTLAND.

The engine driver Dave Hewitt beside his charge, the 'first steam motor car in Scotland'. Catrine Station opened in 1903 and ran for forty years, not counting its temporary closure to passengers during the First World War. By the early 1940s there were only three trains a day and the line closed to passengers permanently when it became evident they couldn't compete with the frequent and cheap services run by the buses. It was reopened for one expensive PR operation in 1957. It took thirty men three days to make the line useable for a Sunday School trip to Girvan for five hundred kids.

Catrine Church was built in the 1790s as another piece of Sir Claud's moral furniture. However, there was no parish graveyard until the 1830s and this adversely affected the population records. Parents often didn't register births and, because people were buried elsewhere, there was no record of deaths. The area around the church was eventually allowed for burials but is now in a bit of a state. The rusted remains of a Victorian gas light are rotting near the entrance and many of the grave stones are making their way down to Mill Street. A quick look at their inscriptions reveals the graves of the old carding master and various managers. But most poignant is the number of child graves. Three children here, all dead by the age of ten, belong to the Morton family and further investigation reveals that all the other members of the family had lived only to their early fifties.

RIVER AYR
CATRINE

Cows being led down the road from St Cuthbert Street towards Ayr Street. The rounded house leading into Wood Street once belonged to the Doak family, a member of which emigrated to Canada, became a famous doctor, and ended up having Doaktown named after him. The chimney in the background belongs to the brewery.

Repairs to Reid's Pool in the 1920s. The Pool is close by the road up to the voes and has a weir made up of three eight foot steps which slowed down the flow of river. The Ayr is the second-fastest flowing river in Scotland and its current was so strong that it had washed away the steps and part of the retaining wall by the time this picture was taken.

203/105

Wood Street, Catrine.

Wood Street today is almost unrecognisable from this turn of the century shot as most of its buildings, including the Doak house on the left, have gone. New flats straddle Wood Street and Ayr Street and much of the tenements on the left hand side have been demolished.

WOOD STREET, CATRINE.

Wood Street, looking up towards St Cuthbert Street voes. The left hand side is now the site of a few private homes and areas of wasteland. The mill square is back to the left with the Bank of Scotland on the corner of Wood Street and St Germain Street. Building societies and banks didn't arrive in towns until the nineteenth century. Before then the masses lived hand to mouth without the luxury of extra money to save. Those who could save could only make do with the Penny Savings banks introduced by the Co-op or the various Friendly Societies and clubs (such as mort cloth unions) set up to help put money aside for essential purchases.

Stewart Place got its name because it was built near to the home of Dugald Stewart - professor at Edinburgh University and friend of Burns. At one point there was a toll house situated here for travellers from Cumnock and Whiteflat. The tenement block was eventually demolished and replaced by a garage, which itself has since been demolished.

In the heydays of the mill the square was the heart of Catrine and shops were crowded into the bottom floors of the tenements surrounding it. The man in the foreground is standing in the shop doorway that used to belong to Cook's Tearoom. Bridge Street leads off a little futher up with the Volunteer Arms (known as the Honky Tonk) on its corner.

Cook's Tearoom with May Cook in the doorway. The tenement block is still standing but the tearoom has been converted into a flat and painted an unfortunate blue.

Sorn village, comparatively unchanged over the course of the past two centuries, provides a good contrast to its once industrial neighbour. Originally part of Mauchline parish, the village came into its own when it was officially separated in the 1690s. The village was initially known as Dalgain after the Esquire of Dalgain, a local noble, but 'Sorn', meaning 'snout' or 'disagreeable visage', was slowly adopted because of nearby Sorn Castle, presumably when the Esquire was no longer around to complain. By the 1790s the village population was about three hundred as it is today, although the ranks of its dead are swelling disproportionately. Having been voted the 'prettiest village in Great Britain' in the mid-eighties it is still attracting some dubious attention with many smitten outsiders asking to be buried there.

Sorn Castle is still standing despite an old prophesy that it would end up half in flames and half in the River Ayr. Dating back possibly to the fourteenth century, when the Keith family built its keep, it was added to and improved on by later owners. During the 'Killing Times' soldiers were stationed at the castle to combat local Presbyterians. One of the latter was the Covenanter minister Alexander Peden, who was forced into hiding in the district and had to live in a cave dug with his own hands. After his death in 1686 the outlaw minister was allowed a grave in the parish graveyard but shortly afterwards his corpse was exhumed by the dragoons for grisly display at Cumnock gallows in a tardy and brutal attempt to make an example of Peden. The story tells that the Countess of Dumfries was so outraged by this act that she managed to get him re-buried at the gallows. This spot was later chosen for Cumnock Graveyard, meaning in effect that the old Covenanter eventually got a consecrated burial and the last laugh.

Since the turn of the century Sorn Castle has been in the hands of the McIntyre family who have made modern alterations such as adding a balcony and creating parking space for motor-cars. During the Second World War the castle was requisitioned by the army. This resulted in a revival of its ghost stories and soldiers sleeping in the gun room often awoke with an attack of the night terrors, although nothing spectral was seen. Pictured here is Sorn Castle Saw Mill which produced wood for sale and to use for estate repairs. Part of its buildings are still standing although the business closed a couple of years ago.

Sorn made its living mostly from agriculture with a little mining, weaving and mill work thrown in. Low populations in the distant past can be attributed to a lack of agricultural advancement. People died of poverty, lack of food and ignorance. This slowly changed as agricultural improvements increased the supply of food available for both humans and beasts. Sorn's entry in the First Statistical Account, written in the 1790s, shows some evidence of this. Although advanced methods of crop rotation had yet to be introduced, local farmers were beginning to lime their soil, take more care with cultivation and improve their breeding methods. Nevertheless, parishioners were still dying needlessly. Its writer spoke despairingly of children dying because they weren't inoculated against diseases such as small-pox. Country people believed in absolute predestination and looked upon vaccinations as an attempt to alter the course of Divine Providence.

Although there were some pits and miners travelled to nearby collieries, coal wasn't a huge concern in Sorn and remained under-developed. One writer actually speaks of some seams at Blackside Hill being partly wrought and then forgotten about. Other potential coal faces were neglected because the fire engine necessary to drain them of water hadn't been acquired. John Lees, a Reynolds and, at the far right, Billy Jamieson are pictured taking a break from boring for coal around the early 1900s. They would have been carrying out a geographical survey for the nearby Dalgain mine, to trace the extent and depth of the coal face. The bore was worked in teams with two men labouring at the handles while the other two rested.

Miners pickaxed a pittance from the coal face in claustrophobic, uncomfortable and dangerous circumstances. Pit owners, by contrast, lived in style. Sir Henry Farquhar's daughters are pictured here at Gilmilnscroft, the family estate. Gilmilnscroft was said to have some of the oldest pit workings in Scotland and in the days before 1799 (when an Act of Parliament was passed outlawing this practice) its employees were apparently sold as property to other pits. The estate changed hands over the years, being owned by a David Somerville who restored it and David Ross the whiskey magnate, as well as also enjoying a stint as a boys private school. Unlike many country houses, Gilmilnscroft has survived and now belongs once again to its original owners, the Farquhar family.

The Alston family working in their smiddy off Main Street. Hailing from Muirkirk, the Alstons established their successful business around the end of the nineteenth century and their busy premises often had up to five fires going at any one time. The business survived until at least the 1950s and the original premises have been taken over as a motorcycle shop. Smiddy's were a fatal attraction for small boys who were drawn in by the smells, warmth and the possibility of stealing carbine from the carbine lights. Small pieces of this could be placed in a bottle and used to set the cork flying off into the air.

Robert Lightbody, Sorn quoiter, pictured here in the early 1900s. Robert worked as a taxi-driver although, along with all the other drivers of the day, he never sat a driving test. The quoiters in the district competed for the grand McIntyre Cup, donated by the owners of Sorn Castle. This prize hasn't been seen since the 1930s when it mysteriously disappeared - perhaps it's now languishing in some Sorn attic . . . . Interest in quoiting died away after the First World War and the club minutes give record of successive attempts at reviving the sport, finally giving up in 1936.

BRIDGEND AND SURROUNDINGS.

Bridgend was just outside Sorn village on the way to Mauchline and housed workers from the nearby Bridgend Tile Works. Most of these rundown and damp dwellings were demolished in the late forties and their inhabitants were re-housed in Catrine. By this time, with decreasing employment opportunities in the village but improved communications, locals were beginning to travel to the factories of Kilmarnock to find work. Some jobs still existed however - the last two mole-catchers in Scotland lived in the village. Although Sorn has seen few physical changes over the years, the Third Statistical Account of the fifties made special mention of accusations then being bandied by the 'old folk'. The village was going down hill and 'the incomers' were blamed for increasing swearing, gambling and Communism!

Sorn School, c.1910. Top row (left to right): Miss Smith, ?, Martha Harrison, Mary Kerr, Lizzie Hogg, Peggy Gibson and Meg Thompson. Bottom row: Sarah Reynolds, Sarah Foster, a member of the McGlauchin family, Nancy Williamson, Meg Cameron, ?, Mary Collins and Milly Halliday. Can anyone fill in the blanks and tell us the exact date?